HERE'S YOUR MARTINI, MR. HOGAN

An Encounter With Golf Greatness

EDWARD D. PAYNE

**CHRYSIPPUS
PUBLISHING**

Here's Your Martini, Mr. Hogan

An Encounter With Golf Greatness

Edward D. Payne

Published by:
Chrysippus Publishing
Arlington, Texas

Typesetting: Raef Payne

Cover Design: Raef Payne

Illustration: Duoc Le, Don Collins

ISBN 13: 978-1-7344602-0-9

Printed in USA

Dedicated to my wife, Sherry,

whose love & support has

endured for over thirty years,

through all the joys and struggles

of this golfer's journey.

Table of Contents

HERE'S YOUR MARTINI, MR. HOGAN

CHAPTER I

A Stunning Reception

Monday, August 13, 1990

An untouched birthday cake that read "Happy Birthday Ben" sat on the table while the old man stared out the window engrossed in an amateur golf tournament. He then turned his attention back to me as I continued to discuss my recent tournament woes.

"Well, after being encouraged by qualifying for the Texas State Open, I drove for two days nonstop to the next tournament in Sioux Falls, South Dakota and nothing worked. I think it has something to do with my timing. Maybe I need to adjust my waggle. What do you think Mr. Hogan?"

His steely grey eyes seemed to bore right through me. He paused before he said, "I think we've been through this exercise before." He paused again. "I'm going to be curt with you. One of these days you are going to be an old man and still not know a goddamn thing. You get up at daybreak, and you hit balls until dark, and if you can't read a golf course you might as well be driving a goddamn gravel truck!"

After absorbing the impact of those stinging words, I quickly redirected the conversation like a sports reporter trying to get the big scoop. "Mr. Hogan, why was that sixth place finish at Oakland such a big moment in your career?"

His tone turned nostalgic as he recalled those days. "For me, $385 was a lot of money. I mean it wouldn't have been that much for some, but it was a lot for me. It was gas money!"

I knew the story about the 1938 tournament in Oakland, California. After being backed in a corner with less than $100 in his pockets, then losing two of his car tires to thieves, Hogan finally broke through, stringing three respectable rounds together, and then shooting 67 in the final round to finish in sixth place.

Then, quietly muttering, as if thinking to himself, Mr. Hogan said, "I'm trying to place you." He withdrew his eyes from mine and returned his attention outside to the juniors finishing up on the eighteenth green.

With that, I said, "Thank you Mr. Hogan."

He replied, "Good luck fella."

As I retreated from the table, I was on one hand stunned that he no longer remembered me, but at the same time grateful that I had been one of the lucky few who'd had the opportunity to benefit from his counsel in his latter days.

CHAPTER II

Unexpected Turn of Events

Mid July 1989

Our paths in life often take certain twists and turns and some of our choices lead to dead ends. But every now and then opportunities that seem to be decisions we make strictly for survival seem to be fortuitous moments in our lives, as if the planets have momentarily aligned to bring serendipitous results.

Looking back, that mid July morning in 1989 when I was scrolling through the local Ft. Worth newspaper employment sections was such a time. The ad read, "Part-time banquet waiters needed, Shady Oaks Country Club, Ft. Worth, Texas..."

But before I continue my story of how I ended up working at Shady Oaks, I have to take you on a slightly circuitous path, starting in the late 1970's and the 1980's, when I began my search for golf glory.

For three years, after graduating from college in the mid seventies, I worked in a golf shop, but my competitive juices were relentless. So I left that life to chase my dream in state opens and eventually, the Canadian Tour. I supported my quest with waiting jobs, some of which paid quite well. Then, in 1983, I traveled halfway around the world to play the Asian Tour. Although the tour turned out to be the greatest adventure of my life, it also was very hot and humid, expensive, and at times miserable and frustrating. I would sweat out all of my electrolytes within a few hours of competition to the point of almost not being able to remember my name.

The only remedy I found to combat the condition was a supplement I heard about in Singapore called Lepovita. However, a few days after this discovery, I happened to play with an American expatriate oil man in Jakarta, Indonesia and the subject of the miraculous power of Lepovita arose. As we marched down the jungle framed 8th hole with caddies in tow, my new friend halted for a moment and with a wry grin overtaking him said, "Yeah, we sent that stuff to the lab and the report came back, 'Your horse has diabetes!' "

For many American players the Asian Tour was the launching pad, or springboard, for the main attraction, the PGA Tour. In my case, I thought it was "do or die." I worked hard, trying not to waste any moments, but I was afflicted by what tour players call "rabbit ears," where one hears tips all day from other players and then tries to implement those many swing keys into his game. The result was that I had a different swing every week. And worse yet, a swing that was guided totally by the left side of the brain, a malady that affects many analytical players.

With the hindsight of forty years, I now believe that the closest I ever came to fulfilling my golf goals was back in my youth when I only had one teacher, and one swing. But the important point to make is that after hitting thousands of balls with one solid technique, then, and only then, could I truly trust my swing and actually turn it over to my subconscious for performing at an optimal level during the crucible of competition. As for my putting in those days, it could be "scary good!"

I had untapped the magical powers of positive thought and piggybacked this with the subconscious when stroking the putts. The result was rolling in nearly every makable putt when the pressure was on. These were the intangibles that I was hanging on to all those years. Moving from those encouraging early days, the ball striking could be quite good, but the putting never came back, at least not with the same consistency.

I returned to the States after a ten week diet of pork porridge, noodles, and shrimp fried rice, owing $6000 to the bank and "Uncle Mastercard," my only winnings a cache of interesting stories. It took two years of selling food to restaurants to get out of hock and build up a little surplus. Although it was great to be solvent again, more and more often, I found myself practicing my golf swing in restaurant bathrooms. Then, with the recession of '85/'86, I was emancipated. I was laid off from my job - a development good for my golf, but a little jarring since I was a recent newlywed.

I had saved some money, and was in a position, however precarious, to once again pursue golf, but there was no question that I needed work. We had my wife's teaching income, but that did not scratch the surface of what we needed to handle all of the bills, not to mention paying for entry fees, motels, gas – all the expenses that go with playing tournament golf. Of all my jobs in and right after college, waiting tables was, without hesitation, my favorite. But, had anyone told me when I was in my senior year in college studying marketing that I was going to relegate myself to food service into my 30's, I would have said, "Just take me out and shoot me and get it over with!" However, banquets seemed to be the best compromise for our situation. I realized that selling food or any other career would require one hundred percent effort a minimum of five days a week. On the other hand, banquet waiting, at least in north Texas, had busy cycles, but then slowed down substantially during the summer and at the beginning of each year. My wife had the summers off, so she accompanied me to the summer tournaments, and I traveled alone to play the winter mini-tour events.

Yet, by July of '89, after returning from an extended attempt on the mini-tour circuit in Florida, the nest egg was gone and I had to step back, assess my situation, and save up some new funds. The reality was, that if I wasn't already at the end of my run, I was close, but I was not ready to quit. I was constantly in hopes that the putter would resurrect itself. Besides, my wife was still supportive, possibly to a fault. I was hired at my old job despite the fact that business was dead in July as usual, so in hopes of finding a temporary lifeline, I looked for new opportunities in the newspaper. That was when I noticed the ad for banquet waiters at Shady Oaks Country Club. Not knowing about the pay cautioned me, but the historic significance of the country club and its association with Ben Hogan had me intrigued.

As I turned into the club grounds for my interview and gazed upon the beautiful landscapes created by the golf course, I couldn't help but flash back to the few times I had played the course as a junior golfer and as an assistant professional. In 1989 Shady Oaks and its golf shop were still distinguished and ranked at the top despite the fact that the number of excellent golf venues had multiplied. But back in the sixties and seventies, it was the gold standard, the loveliest of golf courses, with tees and greens cut to perfection, and wide, rolling fairways as pristine as most course's greens. Where the hills rose in the western horizon lay the par three course where the legend of legends, Ben Hogan, long retired from tournament golf, was known to find sanctuary in his daily practice. The name, Hogan, might have a familiar ring to a non-golfer, but to a golf aficionado it was magical. It was the name of an epic figure who despite almost insurmountable obstacles became practically unbeatable.

As I entered the clubhouse, I was struck by the old, aristocratic ambiance, with a mood set by dark wood walls and hardwood floors. From my perspective, this plush club could rival any of the national clubhouses with their opulent trappings of chandeliers, spiral staircases, and Kashan Persian rugs. But this place was a more intimate setting. To me, it seemed to evoke a sense of elegant, but understated class. Its membership roster included a "who's who" of Fort Worth, many being native Texans with warm hearts and great pride. Upstairs, by the front door, hung two almost life size portraits, one of Marvin Leonard, founder of Shady Oaks, and the other, Mr. Hogan, cigarette in hand.

I hit it off with Herman, the banquet manager, and began working immediately.

CHAPTER III

First Hogan Sighting

A Day in September 1989

Working a charity golf event, perched at my beverage station, bored out of my mind, my eyes began panning the club's periphery, when out of the corner of my eye, I noticed an elderly gentleman, dapper in his gray suit, limping along the asphalt cart path. Although he ambled up with apparent pain, his motion was steady. I recognized the iconic face of Ben Hogan making his way around the curving path toward the Shady Oaks Men's Grill. Just before reaching his destination, he was met by a tail wagging doggy with its ears back, both clearly happy to see one another. Mr. Hogan bent down to greet the excited animal. The more he stroked the pet behind his ears, the more affectionate the canine became.

The bond between dog and master can rival any bond between spouses, mother and daughters, father and sons, brothers and sisters, best friends, or comrades in foxholes. And the loyalty and devotion a master has with his pet is exponentially returned. A dog doesn't care if its master is rich or poor, young or old, famous or unknown, healthy or sick. It will always be there for its benefactor, even by separation of death. After a few heartening moments, Mr. Hogan disappeared into the grill.

CHAPTER IV

The Hogan Tour

Later in September 1989

It was at a luncheon at Shady Oaks Country Club that Mr. Hogan unveiled his new Hogan Tour. The tour, with weekly purses of $100,000 and first prizes of $20,000, compliments of the Hogan Company, was slated to start in February of 1990 in Bakersfield, California. Being the first of its kind, this tour was to provide up and coming pros a training ground for the PGA tour. Although qualifying for this tour was to be in conjunction with the PGA Q School, there would be a total of eight open spots per week that could be earned through a qualifying round before each tournament.

I didn't work that luncheon, so I received my information about this much needed second tour via the next day's newspaper. I took in the tour information, but only have scant remembrance of the rest of the article. I do remember that Mr. Hogan was asked if he had any advice for those competing. "Make sure you don't run into any buses," was his response, a reference to the terrible accident in 1949 that sidelined him from golf for a year and almost took his life.

On a foggy February morning in 1949, the Hogans were driving back home from the western leg of the PGA tour in their brand new Cadillac, just east of Van Horn, Texas when their car was hit by a Greyhound bus that had accelerated to 50 mph in an effort to pass a down-shifted freight hauler while contending with poor visibility. Because the accident happened on a bridge, there was virtually no way to avoid the crash. Had Mr. Hogan not tried to save his wife, Valerie, by throwing himself over her, he would have been crushed to death by the steering wheel as it was driven into the car's back seat.

Doctors first said he would never walk again. Then they said he would never play golf again. His determination proved both prognostications wrong when he won the 1950 US Open at Merion in Ardmore, Pennsylvania. To quote the 18th century English poet, Edward Young:

"Affliction is the good man's shining time."

In the article, he also related a dream he had experienced where he made seventeen holes in one in a row and on the 18th hole his ball flew straight for the hole, but lipped out. "I was so damn mad," he was quoted as saying.

The possibilities the tour offered were like a shot in the arm for me. I hoped that I would be able to qualify to play in some of the Hogan Tour events the next summer.

CHAPTER V

Charles

Late November 1989

Sometime after Thanksgiving I ran into Charles, the day manager of the Shady Oaks Men's Grill, in the employee locker room. We had visited on such meetings over the last months, and I liked him very much.

Charles had come to Shady Oaks at its inception, along with the flag poles, in 1958, and all the members seemed to have the highest respect for him. He was a man of average height and build, whose close cropped, salt and pepper hair, complimented by his coffee complexion, imbued a distinguished appearance in his burgundy vested uniform. He always wore a bright smile and displayed a disarming nature, making him a perennial club favorite.

Knowing that another slow cycle was imminent in January for the banquet scene, I mentioned to him that should he need any help during the winter months to keep me in mind.

CHAPTER VI

The Men's Grill

Wednesday, February 14, 1990

The Shady Oaks Clubhouse was a split level architectural gem. The upper level housed posh banquet rooms with picturesque verandas. The lower level consisted of a chain of rooms beginning with the golf shop in the northeast wing and ending at the building's southwest wing with the very comfortable Men's Grill. The grill was walled in glass on its respective south and west sides, and was distinguished in that it was the only room on the property that was exclusively for men during the day, but transitioned into a family venue in the evenings. It had become a favorite watering hole and card parlor for many of Ft. Worth's movers and shakers.

I had worked a few evening stints in the Men's Grill in January, but this Wednesday would be my first day shift, and I knew I would be waiting on Mr. Hogan. While working night shifts, I had occasionally seen Mr. and Mrs. Hogan come and eat in the stately, more formal dining room. He was cordial, always returning a greeting or salutation, as would Mrs. Hogan.

As far as serving Mr. Hogan, I had an idea as to what he expected from the waitstaff. I had heard tales of perfection seeking in days of yore such as him sending his scramble eggs right back to the kitchen if they were too runny or dry, but these days he was considered generally easy to serve. During the Hogan's visits to the main dining room, he might occasionally complain that the room was too dark to read the menu, or that the room was too cold. But those were legitimate complaints. He was not known to be a high maintenance customer. However, in order to make sure that he did not have any peccadilloes, or things that might offend him, I inquired of a fellow waiter as to his likes and dislikes. He didn't mention any concerns, but offered an observation. "The thing is, he can go out on you."

"What do you mean?" I asked.

Then he went on to tell his story. "One day I served him a martini and after many minutes and many sips, I noticed that except for melting ice cubes, the drink was finished. I went over and asked Mr. Hogan if he was ready for another martini. He didn't react in any way, but continued to stare ahead in a catatonic-like trance. After a few more attempts, I addressed him even louder to try to break the spell. As if awakening from a hypnotic state, Mr. Hogan exclaimed, 'Oh, sorry, I was playing the ninth hole!' "

But on this day, he was definitely not in any concentrated funk. In fact, he was quite animated, raving about his new tour and its whopping $20,000 first prize. He said that the largest purse he ever played for in one tournament was $12,500. "If I had won $20,000 at one tournament, well, I might have retired!" he exclaimed.

After lunch, he set out on what I later would observe was an almost daily ritual trek onto the golf course.

CHAPTER VII

Navy Bean Soup

Saturday, February 17, 1990

This particular Saturday morning, with the temperature hovering around a chilly 38 degrees, Charles, the day manager in the grill, did not mince words when Mr. Hogan arrived. "The temperature might not reach 50 today," he declared.

"It's going to kill us!" Mr. Hogan exclaimed. He dropped into his chair, and flashed the bartender a thumbs up sign, which was Hogan code for a Smirnoff vodka martini, extra dry, on the rocks. The drink, complete with a two olive garnish, was delivered by Charles.

He nibbled away at the olives, which were his amuse-bouche before lunch, and then settled into a more pensive mindset. However, his momentary solitude was quickly broken by the arrival of his brother, Royal, who was joining him for lunch. Soon after the order was taken, the food, a steaming cup of navy bean soup for Mr. Hogan and a club sandwich for Royal, was promptly expedited to the table. As the soup was served, my mind jogged back to Wednesday's shift and it occurred to me, "Didn't he order the same soup that day too?" What I came to realize was that navy bean soup would be his constant staple during my brief tenure there.

Royal ate at a normal pace, but Mr. Hogan, without question, was one of the slowest eaters I had ever seen! I wondered if he had trained himself in such meticulous manners to even further improve his golfing prowess. After all, I had heard that he had advised a fellow pro to shave and drive slowly on tournament days. To carry this routine over to dining room habits made all the sense in the world.

My mind returned to Wednesday's image of him wearing his fedora and carrying a golf club, heading out onto the course. I wondered if he might go out on another excursion after lunch, but since Wednesday was at least twenty-five degrees warmer, my gut feeling was no, as it was becoming clearer and clearer how much he abhorred cold weather. Perhaps he would instead hunker in the warm grill and watch the die hards practice.

His table, located in the southwest corner of the room, provided the most panoramic view of the classic golf course. Since it was February, much of the course's seasonal, emerald majesty was absent due to winter's plunder, but the wide fairways with their many swales and slopes, accompanied by fully blooming live oaks adorning their borders, were still pleasing to the eye. The tacit observer might wonder if a player was ever left with a level lie on the rolling fairways.

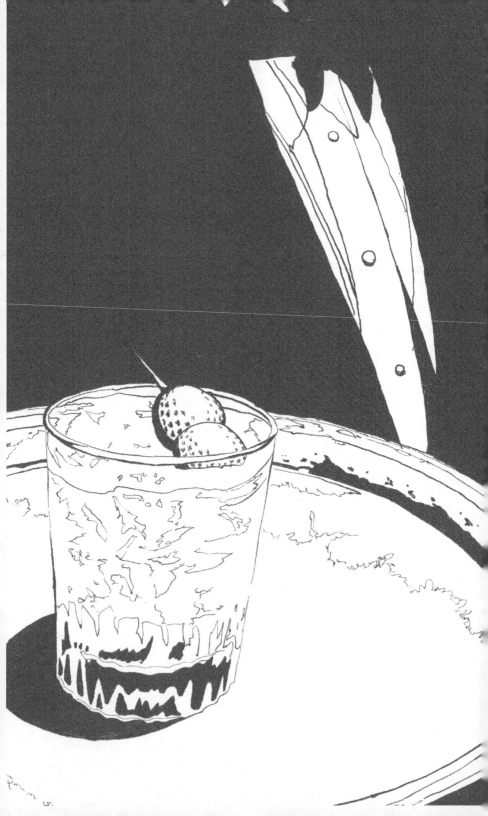

CHAPTER VIII

Breaking The
Ice

Sunday, February 18, 1990

From a waiter's perspective, of all the senses that can best be retrieved, the olfactory, or sense of smell, would rank at the top of the list. All the wonderful aromas permeating from the kitchen, from bacon and eggs in the morning, to the flame kissed charbroiled burgers at lunch, and the tantalizing prime cut steaks in the evening, continue to waft in my memory. The complimentary garlic and buttery melba toast that was placed on each diner's table was as delicious as any this side of the Mississippi.

The "Hogan" round table, which was an eight chair seating, was unique in that it was the only one in the room that had a lazy susan attached to the center of the table. By deploying this device, a guest could grab the salt or pepper, or any other condiments, with a simple rotation of the base, thus alleviating any need for interrupting a line of conversation during a meal.

Mr. Hogan arrived around eleven or so in his weekend regalia consisting of a golf shirt, cashmere sweater, and pressed slacks. As a general rule, that early in the day, with the exception of the gin rummy players, a cabal of six to eight distinguished members, he had his side of the grill to himself. That was the case when I greeted him and placed his martini in front of him. As he gazed out the window, I wondered if it would be best to leave him to his thoughts. However, I was curious to hear his views on the development of his new Hogan Tour.

Breaking the ice, I inquired, "Mr. Hogan, how is your new tour going?"

Still focused outside, he took a sip of his drink, and then returned it to the table, jangling the ice cubes as he set down the crystal glass, and replied, "Very well!"

Though feeling a little nervous, I continued, "A tour like this has been needed for a long time. It's a wonderful thing! In fact, I'm hoping to try to qualify for some of the tournaments this summer when they are in a reasonable proximity."

At once, his head and body sort of swung around. His eyes studied me with an inquisitive look. He paused for what seemed like forever before saying, "One of the assistants said he was going to try to qualify at Portland." Having already studied the schedule, I knew that one of the first events was in Portland, Texas, a small town near Corpus Christi, in south Texas.

I interjected, "I thought about that one, but really, there is no way I could get ready that quickly. It would be ludicrous to try. Didn't you once say that if you missed three days of practice, it would take you six weeks to get your level of execution back?"

"That's right, playing golf is a 24 hour a day job. You've got to get yourself in shape to play."

"You mean by getting your legs really strong?"

"No, I mean you must play the courses on

which you are about to qualify two or three times before the qualifying round." Then he exclaimed, "Man, there are so many good players now."

"You're right," I agreed. "The mini-tours are like little tour factories. And they are all playing these metal woods and Ping Eye II irons. There must be something to them." I was one of the few remaining purists with ten year old forged Wilson Staff muscle back irons, and a persimmon Tony Pena driver whose size was all of about 150 cubic centimeters. Today's drivers max out at 460 cc's, more than three times the size of those used in the fifties, sixties, and seventies.

After taking another sip of his drink, he said, "You need to find a club you can play and forget the rest."

Then, further pleading my case as to the difficulty of the impending task, I said, "There were two hundred qualifiers for eight spots in Bakersfield."

Without blinking an eye, the great possibility thinker said, "You must devote all your time to get yourself ready so you will be one of the eight."

I responded with a nod.

Finally, with a slight smile, he said, "Good luck fella, I hope you make it." And with that, he took another sip and nodded to his brother, Royal, as he arrived. Then the day got busy.

CHAPTER IX

The Triple Crown

Sunday, February 25, 1990

It had been a week since I had last worked in the Men's Grill, but surprisingly, Mr. Hogan picked up where we had left off. Perhaps he actually liked having a golfer/waiter around. During the few times I played at Shady Oaks as an assistant pro, we were admonished that if there happened to be any Hogan encounters, we should just leave the man alone. However, I was now in a position to see the other side of Mr. Hogan. He might not have liked to be approached on the course, but in this setting, he couldn't have been more cordial.

After I placed his drink on the table, Mr. Hogan initiated the conversation. "The largest purse of any tournament that I ever played in was $12,500." A reminiscent smile crossed his face. "I was usually playing for fifty bucks just to get to the next town." This comment reminded me of an amusing story I had heard of Hogan and Jimmy Demaret when they played a practice round in Florida during the early years and purposely aimed their drives over the fences so they could fill their bags with oranges from the groves when they retrieved their balls.

Almost wistfully he said, "I wish I had a tour like this (Hogan Tour) when I was playing."

I wanted to hear more about his tour, but a question popped in my head that I wanted to ask him. "Mr. Hogan, in 1953 after winning the Masters, US Open, and the British Open, why didn't you play in the PGA?"

"Because the British Open and the PGA were the same week, and besides, I had already won two PGA's," he responded. That seemed strange to me because in contemporary times the Masters, the US Open, the British Open, and the PGA are considered the four "major" tournaments. There would never be such a scheduling problem nowadays.

It should be noted, every golf era has its marquee events which are considered "major" tournaments. For example in 1930 after Bobby Jones had won the British Open and the British Amateur, New York City gave him a hero's welcome with a ticker-tape parade. Then

Jones won the US Open at Interlachen and the
US Amateur at Merion to complete golf's un-
precedented Grand Slam for those days. In
1953 after winning the British Open to add to
his Masters and US Open victories, Hogan was
equally rewarded with a parade down Broad-
way to City Hall in celebration of what was
considered the "Triple Crown." As a footnote
to Mr. Hogan's magical year of 1953, he almost ran the table in his appearances, winning five out of six tournaments. The non-
win was at an unofficial event at Sam Snead's
home course at The Greenbriar, in West Vir-
ginia. Sam won and Hogan placed third.

"Did you ever play any of the holes backwards when you were playing practice rounds
at Carnoustie preparing for the British Open?"
I probed.

He answered with a defiant, "Not true!"

If I had asked him if he had played any of
the holes mentally backwards from green to
tee, I probably would have gotten a different

answer, but he gave me an honest answer to the question I had asked. Then again, it could be that the idea that he played holes backwards was just part of the Hogan mythology.

Changing the subject again, I said, " I watched you play the seventh hole of the last round of the Colonial tournament in 1967. Your approach shot was a long iron that covered the pin. Do you remember that shot?"

He answered by shaking his head, "No."

He may not have remembered the shot, but for me, there was total recall. Sunday's final round was very cool and windy for the month of May. The prevailing south wind had shifted the night before when a norther came gusting through. As a result, the Colonial seventh played dead into the teeth of the wind. He carefully surveyed the situation, took a drag off his cigarette, then exhaled, noticing the smoke as it circled and then drifted behind him. Assuredly, he pulled what appeared to be a three or four iron out of his bag. He flicked his cigarette aside, addressed his ball, took a couple of waggles, and rhythmically swung the blade. During his backswing through the transition to his downswing I felt like I was witnessing Newton's motion law of action/reaction being perfectly demonstrated. At contact, the ball exploded off the carbon steel club face, echoing a sound of impact that was more solid, crisper, and louder than mere mortals could produce. The small sphere soared, curving ever so slightly, before homing in and descending towards the pin. The ball took one hop forward, then stopped, nestling a few feet from the hole as the crowd erupted with adulation. Moments later, the same onlookers would sympathetically groan as he missed the short putt. By this time in his career, putting had become his Achilles' heel.

I suspect the reason why Mr. Hogan could not remember that shot was because it was just one of the many great shots he had hit that week. In fact, the editor of "Golf Digest" was dispatched to Colonial that week to watch all of Hogan's shots and rank each one of them.

The assignment was to assess the accuracy of each shot, with the goal of determining if Hogan was indeed the greatest ball striker ever. After the results were tabulated, of the 141 shots he had executed from tee to green, 139 were judged to be excellent to superb. Of the two shots that were missed, one drive missed the fairway by five yards and an approach shot missed the green by another meager five yards. He finished in third place, though he could have had his sixth Colonial victory had his putter cooperated at all.

Continuing with our conversation, I remarked, "I remember that your swing was faster and flatter than the rest."

Displaying a subtle, half smile, he responded, "The swing must be fast coming through the ball."

After lunch and coffee, taking advantage of another pretty seventy-five degree February day, Mr. Hogan grabbed his golf club and donned his fedora for another outing.

He returned to his inner sanctum in the grill forty-five minutes later. As he stood in front of the TV, located on a wall at the end of the bar, watching the golf tournament while gripping and re-gripping the handle of the five iron in his left hand, I noticed that he seemed larger than before his walk, as if his lungs, arms, and the rest of his body had expanded. It was quite apparent how important getting out on the course was for him, physically and mentally.

As the tournament drew to a close, he exited the grill to return his club to his bag and then went directly to his table. Before taking his seat, he searched the hazy room, bathed by the light of the glaring, setting sun, then, like an Indian scout, placed his left hand flat over his brow, squinted, pursed his lips, and tried to communicate his order to the bartender by raising and lowering a thumb's down signal. Acknowledging his request, I delivered a Glenellen Chardonnay in timely fashion.

"How did you hit them?" I asked.

"I don't play golf anymore," he retorted.

His reply shocked me. I couldn't believe that perhaps the greatest ball striker of all time no longer hit golf balls! I would later learn that he had suffered damage to his left eye during the infamous head-on collision with the Greyhound bus. Although he actually played some of his best golf after the wreck, over time, his depth perception was greatly affected, thus frustrating his golfing efforts.

Moving on, I again mentioned the upcoming Hogan Tour stop near Corpus Christi. His eyes lit up a little when he described the two tour vans that accompanied the tour. "One will repair clubs and the other will contain soft goods," he said.

Jocularly I asked, "Are you going down there to review the troops?"

In a deadpan tone he said, "No, they will be fine without my help."

I thought, "Man, what a thrill it would be for the competitors if he were to show up at one of the events!"

CHAPTER X

Preparation for Tournament Play

March 3, 1990

On this beautiful, clear, Saturday, Mr. Hogan seemed genuinely enthused, if not down right effusive, as he schooled me in the art of competing in golf. I considered myself lucky that there were hardly any other members to wait on at this time, and I could actually stand there and glean from his perception of what is required to prepare for tournaments.

From the short period that I had been around the man, if I had to sum him up in two words, they would be honest and passionate. In citing one of the many examples I could bring up to support his upright character, I reflect on an evening shift I did in the grill in January. Upon my arrival, I noticed Mr. Hogan watching a golf tournament while waiting for an order "to go." When the waitress appeared with his order he signed the ticket and then, almost in a whisper, said, "Thank you, and please remember to charge me for the order I left with yesterday."

"What do you mean, Mr. Hogan?" she inquired.

Clarifying, he said, "I mean, I took an order with me yesterday and I'm afraid I didn't sign for it."

Understanding his point, she said, "Oh, thank you Mr. Hogan."

As for his passion, I could see it in his eyes. He certainly didn't have a one track mind, but when the subject of golf came up, even in the most generic sense, his eyes would light up.

I had just placed his martini on the table when Mr. Hogan adamantly pointed to the practice tee through the window and said, "That's a business out there! When you step up to the first tee, you are the Chairman of the Board." I didn't have any experience as a CEO, but I did have a bachelors' degree in marketing, and had studied some great CEO's. Managing risks, implementing strategies, and adapting to changing circumstances are invaluable skills for golf as in business.

Perhaps realizing that I probably hadn't

experienced being a CEO, he changed his example to a more relatable comparison. "You've got to school yourself. Just like you start with elementary school, then secondary school, then college, then Master's, then Ph.D."

I quickly tried to calculate what level of golf I had achieved. If he was a Ph.D., I was still an undergraduate.

He continued, "And you prepare yourself for the test just as you prepare to take tests in school. You must read a course the way you read a book. You do this by playing some practice rounds and see where to play the shots with the best averages. After four days, that would usually get them."

I assumed that by "them" he was referring to the competition.

Continuing to elaborate he said, "You need to be working all the time, seeing the pin positions before you play." I understood that to mean that, when competing, as you pass one green, while playing another hole, to take note of the pin position, and when playing a pre-tournament practice round, to be mindful of the possible tourney's pin positions. I was also beginning to understand more clearly why he always seemed to be in a cocoon when he competed. He was always working and thinking!

He went on, "For example, look at where the pin is on hole eighteen. The pin position dictates where you want to put your drive. When playing the practice round, you need to read the green so that you know the best spot to put the ball, and then try to do it."

Reflecting back to our previous conversation, I surmised that he did, in a tactical way, play the holes backwards. He started with the pin position and undulations of a green, then fashioned his approach shot so that it would leave an uphill putt. The ball placement could be the difference in three putting or one putting.

"You need to weigh your game against the course. That's how you score," he exhorted.

In trying to digest all of this information at once, feeling a little overwhelmed by his advanced thought, I interjected, "It seems like I've just been pounding the balls in hopes of grooving a swing."

He interrupted, "You're probably practicing ass backwards. I've never hit the same shot twice in my life! You need to hit all of the shots. Every hole dictates the shot. It's a study in preparation. You hit the shots on the practice tee and then take them onto the course."

I believe he was saying that I should be well past the mechanics of the swing, and to have practiced all of the possible shots on the practice tee before beginning the tournament. In doing so, I would have the muscle memory and skill to focus on shaping the shots and managing my game when it came to competition.

Taking my game to the course was not always that easy. In fact, I saw golf as a three rung tier: the first level was practice golf which always yielded a second chance to correct misfires; the next level was on was on the course golf, where the objective was to score with one ball; and finally, there was tournament golf, where the golf demons have humbled many a competitor. Of course, Mr. Hogan, who was a true champion, consistently rose to the occasion at any level because he had a purpose for every shot, whether it be practice or competition, as well as the focus, composure, and confidence to perform optimally in all settings.

I wondered if he had more than one option of how to play a hole.

"Did you have a position a, b, and c?" I asked.

"No, you're always working. Just hit the shot the hole requires. You play the law of averages."

My analysis from this remark was that I should develop my game with high percentage shots to avoid disastrously big numbers on a hole which could result in early elimination in a tournament.

Then his face transformed from a serious look to a more light hearted mood. Displaying a Irish wry grin he said, "I can beat a driving machine to shit!"

"What do you mean?"

"Because it only has one speed."

I recalled a story I had heard about an outing he had with his buddies at Shady Oaks. After hitting a six iron on a par three, he was asked what club he had used. He told them that he had hit a six iron. Then he went back to his bag and pulled out another club, hit it, and said, "I hit a seven iron." Then he grabbed another club and after striking another ball said, "I hit a five iron." The three balls were clumped together. One of the witnesses who related this story to me said that the most amazing thing was that there was no perceptible changes in any of the swings. His marvelous hands, and vast repertoire of shots, allowed him to hit any shot he wanted, with any club, practically any distance.

Then Mr. Hogan likened golf to playing a musical instrument, saying, "Like playing a clarinet, you have soft notes and high notes." Anyone who has read Mr. Hogan's book, *Five Lessons: the Modern Fundamentals of Golf*, would know that he incorporated the waggle into his swing with one of the functions being to expand his shot repertoire. In this classic manual he cites using a rapid, firm waggle for executing hard driving shots and implementing an easy, slower waggle for hitting soft feathery shots. I guess that is what he meant by soft notes and high notes. The comparison of the swing to a woodwind instrument was a new perspective for me. The musical analogy of tuning a guitar where the tension is adjusted to produce the desired tone was more familiar. However, I could understand that any musical comparison could be useful as the coordination of movement and rhythm are necessary for both golfers and musicians.

"Did you ever play the clarinet?" I asked.

"Yes, for a while."

"That's what my wife played," I added. Staying on the spouse subject, I said, "Having married somewhat late in life, I've found that marriage provides a great support system, but with that comes many responsibilities."

He nodded in agreement.

I know that he would concede that his wife, Valerie, provided him with all the support he needed. In my opinion, she was a huge factor in all of his success.

While on the subject of family, I couldn't resist the urge to tell Mr. Hogan about when my three year old son saw a picture of him with Byron Nelson. The tot pointed at Mr. Hogan and said, "Johnny Carsey!" Mr. Hogan grinned in amusement. I have to concede, he did look a little like Johnny Carson in that picture.

Getting back on task, he said, "They were all so good, I would have to beat them (his competitors) with the law of averages. These days anyone who can play a lick can make a darn good living out there."

To me, making it through Q School seemed harder than going through the "eye of a needle." I declared, "Well, it seems awfully hard to me."

He responded, "Of course it's hard. Anything worthwhile is going to be hard."

"You hit it pretty far, didn't you?" I said, invoking the power factor.

"Not particularly," he countered.

Even though he did not consider himself a long hitter, the fact was, that when needed, he could bomb his driver three hundred yards with a persimmon wood driver and a balata ball. Imagine what he could have done with today's equipment!

Peering through the window with a nostalgic look, he reminisced, "Motels used to cost $5 and now they are $100. I remember many times in the middle of the night a motel manager would knock on my door with a complaint from the room next door because of a plop, plop, plop noise, which was me practicing my chipping."

Switching gears a little, I asked, "Do you think you had the best concentration?"

Stoically he answered, "I don't know."

"If I am waiting tables and I am not paying attention or I'm talking, I'm liable to spill something or knock a glass over, and yet Trevino chatters all the way around the course."

"That's his style," he surmised.

In my opinion, Trevino constantly chattered to keep relaxed. That method made it easier for him to then transition to a focused concentration just before a shot. Contrastingly, Mr. Hogan immersed himself into a deep concentrated state and maintained this attention until the last putt found the bottom of the cup.

Continuing, I said, "It seems that sometimes during tournaments my concentration starts to wane, particularly on the back nine."

"Maybe you're getting a little lackadaisical," he suggested.

Curious to know his thoughts on an Asian philosophy I had heard of for developing a proper mindset I said, "When I played in Thailand I met a monk who said the goal was to never be happy, mad, glad, or sad."

He nodded in agreement, but made no comment.

Finally, I brought up a concern I had during competition while waiting for my turn to putt. "Back when I could putt, I would squat down on the edge of the green while mentally psyching myself up to see the line and make the putt, but now I'm afraid I'll get in the competitor's way and distract him."

With jaw clinched and lips tightened, he railed, "Let them get out of the way!"

This would be the only time in all my days of service to the legend that I would see this pugnacious, competitive side of him.

CHAPTER XI

It's A Simple Game

Friday, March 9, 1990

Generally, any agreement to work a shift at Shady Oaks came after examining the demands of my other two more lucrative jobs. However, this week I made an exception because Charles, the manager, was planning to travel to Austin to watch his Dunbar basketball team compete in the Texas High School Championship. In light of this special request, I set aside Friday, Saturday, and Sunday to devote to Shady Oaks. Little did I know the opportunity this arrangement would present.

When Mr. Hogan, in a gray suit, arrived at the grill on this balmy, breezy, Friday, there were already a good number of golfers on the practice tee. For watching golf swings, he definitely had the prime spot. Other than having to look past the gin players, who were juxtaposed at tables along the south window, all he had to do was swivel a little left to observe the golfers on the practice tee, going out off the tenth tee, or approaching the ninth green. His view straight on allowed him to watch the players finishing up on eighteen.

Watching golfers, as he was doing when I brought him his martini, was clearly one of his favorite pastimes. "Do you ever see any good swings?" I asked.

"Sometimes," he replied. Then changing the subject while looking out the window and pointing to the pin position at eighteen, which was front, right, he said, "With the pin placement on eighteen, your drive should favor the left side of the fairway. It gives you a better shot into the green."

Obviously, he was saying that from the left side of the fairway, he could hit a little cut or faded iron shot that would buffet into a right to left crosswind allowing the ball's flight to be basically straight.

He continued, "You are always weighing your game against the course. For example, when short hitters like Johnny Revolta and Paul Runyon played longer par fours, they would sometimes lay up on their approach shots in order to give them a good position for chipping or pitching on their third shot. Since the wedge was a strong suit of theirs, they thought laying up was a higher percentage shot than possibly hitting their three woods in the trap or worse, out-of-bounds."

Then pointing to number nine, he said, "When the pin is in the back, right corner, behind the trap, that position is a son of a bitch to get to! You have to hit the ball really high to get it close." The green in reference was a yawning, kidney shaped, one hundred foot long surface, with the general undulation running down from back to front, although it leveled to a plateau at the back. Since that hole usually played downwind, I recognized how important it would be to hit the ball high just to get it to stop on the green when going for such a pin placement.

"In your book, you said that practicing in a left to right crosswind could ruin a swing. Why did you say that?"

My first thought was that constant practice this way could result in developing a come-over-the top flaw. On the other hand, this sort of wind might encourage a hook like the one that almost put him out of business. All the same, I was not prepared for his answer.

"I forgot!"

It was as if the curtain had been pulled, exposing the wizard. Maybe I didn't pose the question in a way where he could understand, or maybe the question just caught him by surprise, but he just continued on topic. "You have to be able to handle the wind. There are all kinds of winds, and you have to know how to cope with them."

Being a golfer in Texas, dealing with winds was something I knew a little bit about.

Gusting winds require adjusting trajectories, while curving the ball into steady crosswinds can keep the ball from being carried away by the wind, and riding a crosswind when using drivers and fairway woods can maximize distance.

After finishing a cup of coffee, which was often the order of the day for capping off his lunch, Mr. Hogan changed into golf clothes and embarked on his daily walk, this time toting a black driver. As his image receded into the distance, I watched as he trudged along, occasionally stopping to do some golf calisthenics of mini-squats. He would then rotate his right arm holding the club in just the one hand. It looked like he was practicing his take- away.

Within the hour he returned to his padded chair, slightly out of breath, revitalized, and serene, as if he'd just visited with the Holy One on the mount.

As I served him the chilled Chardonnay, he turned a bit and looked at me and said in his baritone voice, "When you step up to the first tee, you're the general. You follow me?"

Being somewhat of a history buff, I could relate readily to a golf champion as a general.

Just like Mr. Hogan, a capable general weighs his options by thinking through the odds of cause and effect in each course of action before he engages in battle. I reflected on the warriors' traits that also could be included in a champion's profile. I had, in fact, studied some of the great generals' finest hours. I was reminded of General George Washington's crossing the Delaware on Christmas Day to defeat the surprised mercenaries representing the British Crown at Trenton, and soon thereafter, transforming his ragtag Continental Army after winning the battle of Princeton. But this became a war of attrition, and although the great general lost many more battles than he won, he was very patient and waited for the decisive battle at Yorktown that won the war.

Such patience and the out-thinking of his rivals were identical traits Hogan exemplified at the U.S. Open at the Oakland Hills and Oakmont venues. Preparation, perseverance and not forcing matters by taking high risks enabled him to win four Opens; and equally impressive, to finish in the top ten in this coveted tournament every time he teed it up from 1940-1960. I thought of all the other noble traits both a great field marshall and champion possess: a fearless nature, knowledge of the terrain, improvisational skills, grace under pressure, and the ability to make quick, sound decisions in the "fog of war." All are necessary for success on either field of competition. I wondered how many of these traits were innate, and how many could be developed.

He continued, "The key is the lie. After reading the course, you not only consider the best angle to the pin, but you consider where you can get the best lie."

Although I obviously had a much more novice approach, I reflected on how many of the championship courses yielded a much wider landing area and sometimes a better lie with a three wood distance as opposed to a narrowing of the hourglass should the player elect to hit his driver. Almost in exasperation,

I said, "I hear what you are saying, but it's the execution that I'm worried about."

He paused for a moment, then responded, "If you can't hit the shots son, go the hell to do something else."

As I was leaving his table in pursuit of taking care of other members, I said, "I'm hoping this new invention I've constructed will help me work the bugs out of my swing."

After catching up with refills and clean up of the other tables, I came back to check on Mr. Hogan. Speaking in a softer tone, he asked, "What's this invention you have?"

"Oh, I've figured out a way to see myself swing while looking in the direction of the ball."

"Well, I'll agree with that," he acknowledged in conveying that it is useful to be able to look at the ball or its direction when using a training aid.

At that point we got a little busy with the finishing groups from the eighteenth hole.

Soon afterward, I noticed that a fellow member had joined Mr. Hogan and was asking for golf advice concerning a particular swing flaw. Mr. Hogan raised his seat slightly out of the chair while exclaiming very audibly, "So many swing like this," exaggerating an over-the-top and lunging move by bobbing his head forward while simulating a swing. Lowering himself back into the chair, he kept repeating, "The game is so simple. If this chair didn't have arms, I could hit the best shots in this chair. You wouldn't believe it!"

While saying this he was making simulated swings, without any club, with his fast hands lashing through the air. As he swung back, his right arm would fold nicely, with the elbow pointing down and the left arm extended. During the swing forward, his left forearm would begin its counter-clockwise rotation, resulting in the left arm breaking on its way to the follow through, while the right arm extended. In essence, the backswing and forward swing were mirror images. The speed he could generate with his arms and hands was impressive. Every muscle and tendon in his back, shoulders, arms, and wrists was limber.

Continuing with his pupil, he said, "One needs to train himself...." I believe he was advising the student to learn to have the posture and sitting sensation without being so low to the ground. He continued on in a quieter tone saying something about blocks, but I didn't hear the rest of his theory. Of course, as a golfer, my attention was easily grabbed whenever Mr. Hogan talked golf, but I was busy working the room and would never intrude on any of his conversations with the other members anyway.

CHAPTER XII

The Prime of Life

Saturday, March 10, 1990

Mr. Hogan arrived at his usual time for a Saturday, 10:30 or so. As I served him his martini, another member pulled up a chair to visit with him.

Later, I checked back on his drink and found him alone. The urge came over me to ask him a few questions. I began, "When I played my best golf, I had a Vardon overlap grip. I changed to an interlocking grip to gain length, but I seem to have lost some accuracy. I'm now thinking that the Vardon grip is the best grip."

"I agree," he answered.

Looking back, one of my great regrets about these invaluable moments of conversation was that I never asked for an in-depth explanation of his grip. Another waiter related to me how Mr. Hogan once demonstrated the golf grip to him by saying that with the right hand it's like shaking hands with the club with the pressure from the two middle fingers. That seemed pretty simplistic coming from him, but since my waiter friend was not a golfer, perhaps Mr. Hogan was trying to make the grip very simple for him.

Before I go any further, I want to make it clear that he did not always answer when I would pose a question that dealt with the mechanics of the golf swing. Possibly he did not want to confuse me. Possibly he was thinking, "I'll let this young guy dig it out of the dirt." Perhaps he was too preoccupied with the cares of the world. Regardless, there were times when my instincts told me to simply leave him alone. Truthfully, I was quite surprised that he had taken any interest in me at all, especially in light of the stories I had heard of his aloofness and desire for solitude.

After bringing Mr. Hogan a fresh drink, I asked him a strange question about a statement he had allegedly made to a younger pro about how he would practice today if he had it to do all over again. I said, "Mr. Hogan, did you once say that if you could turn back the clock you would focus mostly on your driver and your wedge?"

"You need to practice with all the clubs, hitting all the shots from all of the different lies."

"What about the putter?"

"Isn't that one of the clubs?"

While we were on the subject of putting, I decided to throw in my own two cents while doing a little name dropping. "Although Mr. Nelson recommended that I use both hands at the same pace when rolling in putts, I seem to have much more feel when using my dominant right hand."

He made no comment. It was known that he was a traditionalist when it came to putting styles. He refused to adopt the sidesaddle method that Sam Snead used to extend his golfing longevity. But I am sure that during all of his putting travails, he had tried almost all possible methods to sink putts. In the final analysis, it was probably his ailing knee as much as his dismal putting that convinced him that it was time to end competitive golf. He had re-injured his left knee, which was initially injured in the 1949 accident, at a tournament in Houston in 1971 on a par three hole while making his way down a ravine in an attempt to play a recovery shot after his tee shot had failed to clear the hazard. Nine holes later he withdrew from the tournament because of the instability in this hindered joint. And that was that!

I then asked, "Is it true that you picked the ball clean when you hit your irons?"

"There have been more things said about me that aren't true. I took divots."

Once again, I think if I had asked if he swept his long irons off the ground I might have gotten another answer. A good friend of mine who was an assistant pro under the beloved head pro, Roland Harper, at Colonial Country Club, conveyed to me the machine-like precision of Hogan's long irons by relating a story passed on to him by Roland. The scene took place at Colonial prior to the National Invitational in the late sixties. A frantic member informed Roland that Hogan was practicing his long irons off of the eleventh tee. (The practice tee that bordered the tenth fairway had been overcrowded). Roland hastened his way by golf cart to investigate. The prospect of damage to a tee prior to a tournament was of great concern. Head Pro Harper was amazed and relieved when he reached the site. Mr. Hogan, who had by that time vacated the tee, had left only scant cleat marks. Nary a divot spoiled the surface.

Even though it was still a little before noon, the traffic in the grill was picking up. I left Mr. Hogan to attend to the needs of others. A few minutes later, I returned to his table to deliver his navy bean soup and found him turned around, lamenting over some of his past business decisions to a member seated behind him. He then turned back around to face his table, and I commented, "Mr. Hogan, I can't imagine you making any mistakes in business."

Shaking his head, he soberly said, "I have."

Just before he took his first sip of soup, I asked, "Did you ever think of running for office?"

With no hesitation he retorted, "Politics? Politics will kill you! Hell, politicians will kill you. They want money to get into office, and they want more money after they are in."

I was not sure why he made the first comment, but I could not help from reflecting on JFK and his young life being snuffed out just 48 miles away from Shady Oaks, in Dallas.

After lunch, Mr. Hogan grabbed his fedora and a driver and commenced his walk. As he set out from the grill, just as the day before, he engaged in mini-swings with his right hand fastened to the club, then halted abruptly to do his calisthenics consisting of a series of light squats.

Forty minutes later, while I was walking by the grill's door, Mr. Hogan returned looking more fit and robust than when he had set out for his excursion. He smiled at me as he handed me his club. It was beautiful, with a shiny, black finish on its crown. But it was as heavy as an axe. With great pride, he exclaimed, "This is a weighted club. It will keep your forearms strong."

Handing it back to him I said, "I've got one."

"Oh, good," he responded as he retreated through the locker room door with the club.

It is true, I had a weighted club, but only because I had read in some book that he recommended training with a heavy driver, but I didn't tell him that. As in many other examples of his being ahead of his time, he had a weighted club long before the Momentous weighted club was ever on the market. Even though it was a training club, the sight of the driver, with its beautiful roll and bulge, reminded me of how great Hogan equipment was. For years, his clubs had the distinction of being considered the best clubs in the world.

He deposited the club in the bag room, and then settled into his usual spot. I promptly brought him a Chardonnay and slid it on the table opposite his right hand. He looked up at me with a sincere expression of empathy, stammering slightly, as if to punctuate the important advice he was about to impart. "Son, you, you got to get the edge, hmm, hmm, you follow me? Hmm, hmm?" Then he reiterated what he had told me before, he said, "You read a course the way you read a book, then you play the law of averages. I'd get them almost every time. Sometimes you might get the edge on the seventieth hole or at a different place."

I reflected back to his famous British Open triumph at Carnoustie. I had heard that during the practice rounds he hit three drives on each of the par fours and par fives: one on the left side of the fairway, one on the right side of the fairway, and one down the center to determine the best angles for the various pin possibilities and to discover any soft underbelly, or vulnerable hole, that the course might be concealing. I wanted to ask him if during the tournament's last round he had gotten the edge on the fifth hole when he chipped in for a birdie out of a hanging, sandy lie at a bunker's fringe, or the par five, sixth hole after hitting the gutsy driver down the narrow, OB-bordered, twenty three-yard-wide neck, which allowed him to get home in two for an easy birdie; or if he got the edge on the par three thirteenth after rolling in his birdie for his only deuce of the day. However, other members needed my attention.

The afternoon was quite busy with tea refills, beer orders, lunch deliveries, and the clearing of plates. Out of the corner of my eye, I noticed Mr. Hogan had raised his hand to get my attention. I said, "Yes, Mr. Hogan?"

Mr. Hogan, being particularly loquacious that day, said, "Son, you have to hit the shots that a hole requires. You may not always be able to pull it off, but you've got to try." He continued, "You can't play the whole world. It's like you're aiming a rifle. You follow me? Huh? You've got to narrow this thing down. You follow me? Huh? Huh? God is helping us all of the time, but you've got to put the ball there. Huh? Huh?" he exhorted while displaying a heartfelt grin.

Finally, I responded, "You're telling me all of this. Where the hell have I been all of these years?"

His eyes were almost misting. With pressed lips he slowly shook his head, then he told me, "It takes a long time, son!" After a lengthy pause, he repeated, "A long time."

He could have responded, "Where the hell have you been?" or "Your generation are a bunch of softies and are not worth their salt." But his humble reply demonstrated the humility he felt for having had worked so hard, for so long, to become an eventual champion.

Pundits have said that one must put in 10,000 hours in an endeavor to achieve expert status. Based on the man's work ethic, he probably had logged that many hours in just three years of effort. Considering that it took him nine long years from the time he turned pro until winning the North/South at Pinehurst, which was considered a "major" tournament at that time, my estimate is that he exhausted at least thirty-six thousand hours on his quest to capture his first victory.

While Mr. Hogan was pouring his heart out to me, my eyes were darting around the room checking on other members' needs. Noticing my preoccupation, Mr. Hogan asked, "Am I boring you son?"

"Oh, no Mr. Hogan," I assured him, "but I need to get back to work."

Leaving his table, I resumed my usual routine of working the room. But within moments, Mr. Hogan signaled for me to return to his table. Upon my arrival he asked, "It's none of my business, but what in the hell are you doing here?"

"It's an extra job," I explained. "I work here as a supplement to my other two jobs."

He pressed on, "You tell me that you have a wife and a baby. Do you think this is fair to them?"

"Well, I do need to set a time limit."

With a nod of the head, he said, "I agree." Then he further probed, "If you don't mind me asking, how old are you?"

"Thirty-eight," I answered, somewhat apologetically.

"Oh, you are in the prime of your life!"

"That's not what my mother-in-law says."

"I don't care what your mother-in-law says."

With that exchange I broke away from him, tending to the needs of the others. But no more than twenty minutes had elapsed when Mr. Hogan raised his index finger again, summoning me to his table. Since his wine glass was full, I interpreted his gesture to indicate that he wanted to tell me something else.

"To play tournament golf, you have to be totally dedicated," he lectured.

I nodded in agreement.

"How old are you?" he asked, for the second time.

"Thirty-eight!"

In his response, while shaking his head, he lamented, "It may be a little late to start, son."

I aged more in those twenty minutes than any other twenty minutes of my life.

CHAPTER XIII

The Longest Day

Sunday, March 11

When I started my shift, with the exception of a few of the gin players, all of the other tables were empty. Mr. Hogan entered through the locker room door. He reached his table, lowered himself into his chair, crooked his neck to look in the bartender's direction, and gave a thumb's up signal. Quickly, I dispatched the order, placing the martini on the table. Then I began, "When I was thirteen, on Christmas Eve, my dad gave me the biggest army sack of golf balls I had ever seen. It was the best present, I think, I had ever received."

Mr. Hogan emphatically nodded in acknowledgment as to convey how well he could relate.

"You know," I interjected, "my dad was born in Stephenville."

"Oh, I was born in Stephenville."

"I thought you were born in Dublin." Dublin is a small hamlet near Stephenville, located about seventy-five miles southwest of Fort Worth.

"No, Stephenville."

Thinking out loud I commented, "I guess good people come from Stephenville."

I was beginning to understand the connection that we seemed to have. It was hard to put my finger on it, but there was something endearing about these small town Texas people. Actually, Mr. Hogan reminded me more of my Uncle Jack than my dad. Both were honest and straight forward, and good natured most of the time, while always saying what they meant. In citing an example of Mr. Hogan demonstrating this straight forwardness, I must preface that I was not present at the ceremonial luncheon that took place at Shady Oaks on the misty January day at which this event occurred. The incident was described to me by a co-worker. The gathering endorsed a newly christened course called The Legends which was constructed on an island in the Pacific. To commemorate the course's grand opening, many golfing legends including Sam Snead, Gene Sarazen, Billy Casper,

Chi Chi Rodriguez, Gene Littler, Bob Toski, Orville Moody, and of course Mr. Hogan were present. A photographer from New York was on hand to document the event by snapping a series of photos of the famous golfers while inside the warm confines of the banquet room at Shady Oaks. But as the day progressed, the sun finally started peeking from behind the clouds. Sensing a respite from the earlier inclement weather, the photographer petitioned for a few photos outside. Mr. Hogan respectfully declined the suggestion by responding, "No, we're done for the day."

Incredulously, the photographer blurted out, "You're kidding!"

Mr. Hogan turned, faced the cameraman, looked him square in the eyes and declared, "I'm Henny Bogan, and I always say what I mean!" "Henny Bogan" was the nickname he had given to himself as an alter ego.

Upon returning to his table to check on his drink, I posed the question, "Mr. Hogan, how do you fade the ball?"

"Oh, when I want to fade it, I move my hands this way (rotating his hands counter-clockwise on his imaginary club, displaying a very weak grip). And when I want to hook it, I move my hands this way (now rotating his hands clockwise with his left hand resting on top of his imaginary grip and his right hand on the underside, emphasizing a very strong grip)." Nothing was mentioned about pronation, or fanning the club face open, as the famous article in the 1955 issue of Life magazine had revealed. I would soon recognize that these adjustments were already incorporated in his swing.

Playfully I added, "You know, I once heard that on your backswing you never allowed your right knee to move, and on your downswing you felt like your legs were running at the ball, so I tried it, and kept trying it, and it wrecked my swing for ten years."

The man made no change of expression or

comment, he only paused a few moments and then asked, "Why don't you work in a golf shop?"

My answer to that question had been hashed out through trial and error in previous years. In fact, apprenticing in a golf shop, instead of playing the Florida mini-tours, was my first choice after graduating from college. However, playing Monday assistant pro tournaments led to perpetual frustration. Although some pros, maybe oozing with talent, were able to balance the challenges of working long hours in the shop and competing, with minimal practice time, I found it did not work for me, even though I did have a few good tournaments. Declaratively, I responded, "I've found that food service actually works better for me because even though I can't play much golf now, in the summer I can really devote my time to preparing for and playing in tournaments."

While we were on the subject of vocations, being curious as to what he had done during the interludes that separated his early golfing efforts, I asked, "What did you do when you had to come off the tour?" He glanced up at me as I continued, "I think I heard that you sold cars."

"No, never did."

I later found out that when I thought I had heard that he sold cars, that what was actually said was that he had dealt cards. I also learned that he was a stick man at Top of the Hill Terrace, a secret casino and gambling den in nearby Arlington, Texas.

After his denial, pressing on for more information, I inquired, "Did you work?"

With a facial expression changing as if the tide was shifting, from a complacent look to a determined gaze and clenched jaw, he uttered, clearly, and succinctly, "I worked all my life!"

I remembered hearing about his humble golfing beginnings: getting up early, waking long before daybreak, always looking for an edge, always trying harder than anyone else, motivated by a quest for perfection, while never being a hardship to his mama. His daily, grueling practice regimen that led to bleeding hands was so well documented that it is now the stuff of legend.

"Well," I inquired, "didn't Henry Picard try to help you?" Mr. Picard was the only person besides Marvin Leonard that offered to help Mr. Hogan during the lean years.

Apparently, Mr. Hogan felt indebted to him because he dedicated his first book, *Power Golf*, to him. But instead of interpreting my question as whether or not Mr. Picard had offered to help him out financially, he thought I meant helping him out with his swing.

"Picard followed 'Marrison,' " he replied.

Not getting the reference, I asked, "Who was that?"

"Some guy who couldn't break 90."

I then realized that he was referring to Alex Morrison, an old school golf teacher.

Excusing myself, before walking back into the kitchen, I noticed unusual changes in the atmosphere outside. What had started as a normal, calm, but balmy day was gradually exhibiting an eerie air. The western horizon as viewed from the Men's Grill from time to time had the ominous intrusions of the draconian B52's flying in and out of Carswell Air force Base. In previous wars, these were the deliverers of the maniacal carpet bombing exercises which terrified enemies, but this day it was nature's demons brewing. Weather changes often come from the west and this Sunday was no exception. Fluffy, feathery, bouncing clouds morphed quickly into black, thunderous beasts delivering driving rain, pelting down on the clubhouse with accompanying winds whipping the trees to and fro. It was a fantastic display of nature exacting its wrath with swift precision on the surroundings, reducing sand traps and greens into ponds and puddles. Darkness descended upon the entire property.

I quickly scrambled through the kitchen to the nearest phone to call home and warn my family of the "mother of all storms" headed their way.

When I returned to my post, Mr. Hogan was still sitting by himself, so as I passed by I matter-of-factly mentioned that I had just called home to warn my wife of the approaching storm.

At once, he got up and stole himself away to the men's locker room. I honestly don't know why he left so abruptly, but given the context of our last conversation, it wouldn't surprise me if he had gone to call his wife to check on her as well.

It didn't take the powers that be long to determine that the golf grounds were unfit for play, and the course was officially closed for the day, but the course's closure didn't discourage the gin players and a few other illustrious members from staying around. The general suspension of activity gave the Men's Grill a whole different atmosphere, with a much slower pace.

A friend of Mr. Hogan's named Jimmy, who appeared to be a partner of his in oil and gas, had braved the weather to share the large, round table in the southwest corner of the room with Mr. Hogan and his brother, Royal. Royal left after lunch, but Jimmy remained.

The day ebbed and flowed as if time had deemed to take a day off in accordance with the suspension of course activities. Finally, the televised golf tournament began and the grill became lively in an unusual way.

I'm not certain why Mr. Hogan seemed more at ease on this rain drenched day. It could have been attributed to the fact that the grill was, by then, virtually empty.

Suddenly, as if the golf tournament had awakened desires and cued him to action, Mr. Hogan jumped up out of his chair and with a hitch in his step, marched through the locker room door as if he were a man on a mission. Immediately he returned with his beautiful, shiny, black weighted club. The next few minutes were a sight that given his age, few would ever be privileged to see again. On that highly uncommon Sunday, during that hour, at that moment, the great legend began swinging his weighted driver in the Men's Grill.

He swung ferociously in a tight semicircle over and over with no pause and at full speed. On any day, I would say that he looked ten years younger than his age, but when I saw him swing the golf club, the clock was easily turned back a quarter of a century. Then, after continuous frenetic swinging, as if getting a grip on himself, he finally slowed down, easing to a slower pace before stopping and handing the club to Jimmy.

Jimmy gripped the heavy implement, addressed an imaginary ball, and commenced swinging the club. With Mr. Hogan occupied with Jimmy, I took the opportunity to check on things in the kitchen.

Upon my return through the kitchen's swinging doors, and noticing that Mr. Hogan had reclaimed his driver, I was stunned when he announced, "Jimmy, I've got a waiter I'm going to put up against you. Come over here son!"

There I was, in my waiter's jacket, my mind racing quickly, trying to assess the situation which was both an opportunity and a predicament. There was definitely a conflict of interest. On one hand, as a waiter, it would be very unprofessional to fraternize in such a way. But then again, this was a totally atypical day, in that the total count of souls present in the grill were Mr. Hogan, Jimmy, the gin rummy players, myself, another waiter, a bartender, and a cook. Maybe, I thought, both of my roles, waiter and golfer, had suddenly merged to help me reach greater goals.

Quickly I rationalized, would a playwright disparage suggestions from Shakespeare? Would an aspiring composer withdraw from overtures of help from Beethoven? Would a baseball player throw out hitting tips from Babe Ruth? I accepted the club and took my stance.

Almost immediately, Mr. Hogan noticed something off with my head at address. He inquired, "Is there something wrong with your right eye son?"

I doubt he would have said anything if my head had been turned away from the target like Nicklaus, but having it tilting in the direction of the target before even initiating the swing was very unorthodox. This flaw of mine was also detected at a mini-tour event in Daytona Beach, Florida by one of Byron Nelson's disciples, Bert Yancy, who was a great player in his own right. On his advice, I stuck a piece of tape horizontally under the bill of my cap

Mr Hogan opened up my left foot 45 degrees and squared my right foot 90 degrees in relation to the target line.

to help me level my eyes to be parallel to the ground. Without my cap, I had fallen into old habits.

I straightened my head and he said, "That's it."

After I made a few swings with the heavy training tool, he intervened again. He opened up my left foot to about 45 degrees (in relation to the target line) enabling me to more easily clear my left side. "It's a logical game, son, you are going that way," he said as he pointed to the imaginary target.

Next, he made my stance wider than my shoulders and then dropped my right foot back further from the target line as if I were going to hit a hook while squaring it up to be ninety degrees in relation to the target line. "Feel like you are in running blocks," he instructed.

"Aha," I thought to myself. "These are the blocks he was referring to on Friday. They are running blocks!" To get the total effect, I slid my left hip laterally, slightly to the left, toward the target, which raised it to be a little higher than the right hip and slightly kicked in my right knee while imagining that I was an Olympic sprinter, poised and anxiously awaiting for the starting gun to fire.

After taking a few moments to assure himself that I had digested all of these adjustments, he went to work on my ball position saying, "Bring the club head further up, further." Incrementally I adjusted the club head as he instructed while keeping my hands basically even with my zipper. He admonished me a third time, "Further!"

Man! I felt like the imaginary ball was being positioned opposite my left, big toe. It could be that my explanation is an exaggeration. Perhaps my ball placement was too far back in my stance to start with, but what I described is truly how it felt.

Then in an encouraging tone, he said, "Let her go!"

As an aside to my narrative, I have found that if I employ this ball position on a drive, while maintaining correct shoulder alignment, it reduces distance killing back-spin and produces a higher launch angle.

I made swing after swing while the teacher observed.

Either Jimmy, or one of the gin rummy players, who had then joined him and Mr. Hogan, said, "He kind of swings like you, Ben." A more discerning eye would probably not agree, but hearing such a comparison felt nice just the same.

In my opinion, the only similarities between myself and Mr. Hogan were that we were both right handers and neither of us wore a golf glove. I can guarantee that if I had ten percent of his precision swing, I would have been teeing it up regularly on the PGA Tour instead of carrying martinis on trays.

After a couple more swings, with a feeling of total exuberance to where I thought my chest was going to explode with joy, my instincts told me that we had spent enough time on my lesson. I gratefully handed him the club and stood aside.

He assumed his stance to an imaginary ball, setting up as though he were going to launch a drive through his favorite window. I surveyed his setup as he slightly lowered himself into a semi-sitting position, with his legs flexed, back fairly erect, forearms facing out, while bracing himself in a wide stance with the left foot open and right foot square and back to the target line in imaginary running blocks, which was evident by his right knee being slightly kicked in.

I focused my total attention on noticing every nuance in his movements while trying to take mental snap shots of every swing frame and to burn them into my brain. I only saw one swing from his classic address position. The succeeding swings would start at the apex of his follow through.

Over and over, each in perfect balance, one swing would rhythmically finish and another would begin, backswing, downswing, backswing, downswing. During the backswing, I noted that all of the body parts were connected together as if they were a finely tuned machine. He had total control of every muscle. The hands, arms, and shoulders turned the hips, and the hips pulled the left knee back behind the ball, or where the ball would be positioned, as the left ankle rolled inward. Basically, on the downswing, the whole process reversed as the left leg and left hip unwound moving laterally, while bracing for the chain reaction of the downswing. I theorized that his connectedness, elasticity, balance, and consistency in the proper swing path were the reasons why he could literally go seasons without hitting an un-solid shot.

But then I started noticing some little distinctions that seemed different than some of the golfing how-to manuals. I watched the next swing more carefully, trying to pick up my observing technique a notch. Once again, his hands, arms, and shoulders in sequence fluidly dragged the club head away while he sat on his imaginary stool.

I asked myself, "Didn't the path of the take-away follow the same route as the right handed drill I had observed him doing the last couple of days on his walks?" Although he had been many yards away and it was impossible to see the minuscule movements, it was clear that he was simulating a take-away. Finally seeing him up close, I could examine his technique as the club moved straight back the first couple of inches, then dropped slightly inside, and when the shaft was parallel to the ground, the toe of the club head was up as if he were shaking hands with someone behind him. I kept my focus as he reached the top of the backswing, setting his club perfectly over his right shoulder.

I continued my dissection of his swing. During the initiation of the downswing, there was the famous lateral shift of the hips, with the left ankle rolling back toward the left while simultaneously his left knee set and braced over the ankle, followed by his arms dropping into the ready position with the club now inside while the back of the left wrist went from a cupped position at the top of the backswing to a flat, cocked position. It was a great snap shot of his extreme lagging of the club with the driver well behind him.

As he reached the kill zone, he let out a grunt while releasing all of his energy at the imaginary ball, accelerating the club even faster on a path down the line while simultaneously his hips spun to the left in completion of a semi-circle. His hands, arms, club, and then shoulders followed the hips lead and the momentum of the swing catapulted him around while the arms at last separated from the torso into his unforgettable classic finish: right arm basically straight in its pose; belt buckle facing the target, and right big toe pivoting around.

Next, I focused on his beautiful footwork. The left ankle again rolled in on the backswing, as the majority of the weight shifted to the inside of a braced right leg which maintained its flex and angle all the way to the top of the backswing. During the downswing, the right foot stayed on the ground until the arms dropped into the ready position, then the heel led the toe as the ankle rolled inward while transferring more weight to his planted left foot. His squeaky feet on the hardwood floor revealed how great a role his feet played as leverage points in his swing.

As he continued to swing back and forth, back and forth, and his brow began showing beads of perspiration, I wondered how much of a role the heavy club had played in slowing down his swing. Reflecting back to his heyday, I asked myself, "Wasn't he known for having a buzz saw swing?" All the same, the club speed was impressive. You could hear a resounding whoosh in the hitting zone. It is amazing how light even these lead filled clubs seem when one is on perfect plane. I continued to watch with my eyes fixed to the man hoping to absorb each swing and that each motion would be imparted to me as if by os-mosis or some mystical transcending means.

As he began to wind down, I reflected on how surreal these past few moments had been. If anyone had told me, even six months earlier, that I would be getting a lesson from Mr. Hogan and watching him demonstrate his classic golf swing, which many considered to be the most effective ever, I would have said, "No way!"

In retrospect, there I was, watching every little move in his swing, when in reality, so many of those details had been slowly built into the composite brick by brick. He had con-structed a swing that allowed him to honest-ly say, "The game is so simple, you wouldn't believe it!"

Still amazed by what I was experiencing, I glanced around the room. The immediate im-pact was one of incredulity. The gin players were totally immersed in their gin game, and the one sidelined player was thoroughly enjoying his chili-dog. To me, nothing could be as interesting as watching Mr. Hogan.

Watching him swing was as much like taking a lesson in physics as in golf. It was like watching a tilted weed eater in action. When I was certain he was finished, noticing how winded he was, I came over to him and I marveled, "You were generating more club head speed than me."

"I was swinging as hard as I could, son!" He exclaimed. Then, pointing to the spot his table was occupying, he said, "We ought to put a golf net right there."

As my eyes met the twinkle in his, for one glorious moment, I felt like we were kindred spirits. "You can't tell where a ball is going in a net," I said.

"You know where it's going."

Shifting gears, I asked, "Do you think you hit more golf balls than any man alive?"

"I don't know, but if I haven't, I need to go out there right now and hit some more," he declared, revealing his endearing dry sense of humor, and his undying competitive spirit.

Then he made a more or less ad-libbed, out of left field comment, "I didn't need pin sheets. I knew where the pins were going to be." I honestly do not know if the competitors in his day were given a sheet describing each pin location as they are now, but I reflected on the stories of his lack of interest in Nassau bets during the practice rounds because he was aiming his approach shots at the strategic places he had deduced would be the pin positions during the tournament. "I was delighted to figure it all out," he added. And he did figure it all out, often without the benefit of local knowledge from a caddy. I believe that during his prime, he always made his own decisions on club selection and green reading. There were no yardage books or range finders when he competed. He nailed down the pins by feel and his mastery of ball trajectory.

Then, he imparted a sage's wisdom in proclaiming, "Every shot is a study, and every hole is a new day." The "every shot is a study" part was something he had elaborated on before, but the "every hole is a new day" explained why he was always so focused on each hole, but never disturbed by any bad break or missed shot. In fact, it was never apparent to any observer when Mr. Hogan was competing as to whether he was five under or five over par. Once a hole was finished, it was done. He was on to the next hole. I began to wonder if Mr. Hogan didn't have a mental library cataloged with the tournament courses he played while accurately chronicling each as a book with eighteen chapters.

Word of all the excitement must have made it through the clubhouse grapevine, because soon, after all had settled down and we were back to business as usual, the food and beverage director peeked his head into the grill, appraised the situation, and then left. His appearance in the grill was so unusual that I wondered if, in my ambition, I'd overplayed my hand.

Upon returning from the bag room where he had deposited his club, Mr. Hogan settled down at a table near the bar to watch the remainder of the golf tournament. While waiting for his Chardonnay, I couldn't help noticing Mr. Hogan's reaction, or lack of one, when a Lincoln Town Car television commercial saluted Jack Nicklaus as the "Golfer of the Century." Displaying no change of expression, he just reached for a cigarette.

I delivered his wine and inquired, "When you swing down to the ball, do you want to keep your right heel down until just before impact?"

"Who told you that?" He countered somewhat exasperated. I had read it, although I may have misunderstood it, in Nicklaus' book, but I did not want to tell him that at the time.

So I changed the subject. This time asking, "What about keeping the head still?"

In response, he took hold of my right

pocket and yanked it laterally across my body with his right hand while saying, "Where is the head going if you are going that way?" Indicating an imaginary target. This exercise demonstrated to me that when I lead with my hips on the downswing, the head should stay basically stationary. I swear, if my hip had not followed his movement, he would have ripped off my pocket.

"It's a logical game," he reiterated. To further illustrate the ideas he was trying to convey, he pointed to a large, round, mahogany table beside us and said demonstrably, "If I am set up to go that way, I can knock that table down!"

Searching for an example to which I could relate, I reflected on the seventy-two inch round banquet tables which I rolled into ballrooms for setup and service, and the massive power they possessed when in motion because of their constant center point. If I were to lose one of these tables in transport, it could blow a hole in a wall.

Mr. Hogan paused again, and then with an almost imperceptible shoulder shrug and all the humility in the world said, "Son, maybe my theories aren't right."

I thought to myself as I left his table, "Sir, you wrote the book."

Ten minutes later, upon returning to his table to check on him, I noticed that he was examining the tournament leaderboard. The golfer in first place had a comfortable lead.

"I wish I'd had a three shot lead going into the last round of a tournament," he remarked.

"Would you change your strategy?"

"No, you should know how you are going to play the whole course when you step up to the first tee. Again letting his guard down, he said, "I don't have all of the answers son, but the game must be logical. You set up this way because you are going that way," pointing out the window to an imaginary target.

A little later, as the tournament was winding down, he noticed that one of the local pros was a contender. He smiled at me and said, "We ought to kick him in his koolakwachee!" He said this affectionately, almost playfully, as if to imply, "We need to help this boy win."

I was surprised at how many names of winning golfers he didn't recognize, but if a local pro was competing, especially one that played his clubs, he generally knew of them.

Changing the subject, I asked him what he thought of women golfers.

"I think they are very good. They swing at the ball very well. They are just not as strong as men."

I pressed on, "Do you like to watch women's golf?"

"I like to watch any golf."

Noticing all the water surrounding the

tournament's golf course, which was located on the Atlantic seaboard in southern Florida, he gasped before declaring, "It looks like someone moved a lot of dirt into the ocean. Who designed that course, Dracula?! How do the members play that course?"

I asked him, "Is the reason you are so proud of your design of Trophy Club that it is such an enjoyable course for the members to play?" Trophy Club is located in a community thirty-five miles northeast of Fort Worth. It has the distinction of being the only course Mr. Hogan designed and developed.

"That's right," he asserted, "there's not a blind shot on the course."

I had played the course once, and had to agree. Trophy Club had a number of tee boxes dotting each hole to allow a player to adjust his challenge. To add to a player's experience, the fairways were wide, the greens were fairly large, and although there was some water, it was not overdone. Every thought in his design seemed to take the average player into account.

The clock finally ushered the end of my shift. I bid Mr. Hogan good-bye and clocked out. The most glorious, but longest of days, was over.

CHAPTER XIV

The Next Sunday

Sunday, March 18, 1990

This Sunday, the Sunday after the Sunday when Mr. Hogan gave me the lesson, I was preoccupied with a conversation I had with Charles, the grill manager, when we discussed my schedule. Business had picked up so much at my main job that it was getting more and more difficult to schedule shifts in the grill.

After we agreed on my hours, he added, "I got a complaint about you."

"Oh?" I responded.

"Yeah, the complaint was that you were talking too much to Mr. Hogan."

"Hmm."

"So don't talk to him unless he talks to you," he instructed.

"Oh, okay," I conceded.

So my feelings of paranoia were not un-founded. The way I saw it, it was any member's prerogative if they wanted to cite a grievance. Besides, I had four years in the country club business. I knew exactly how sensitive some members could be.

Mr. Hogan came at his normal hour for a Sunday. I brought him his martini and took the opportunity to thank him for his golf tips the previous week. "Thank you, Mr. Hogan," I said. "I really appreciate the advice you gave me last week. Some of the waiters or other employees may not understand what a gift your suggestions were."

"Well, they don't play golf," he responded.

With that I went to take care of the needs of the other members who were starting to arrive. Unlike the previous Sunday, this was turning out a be a normal, busy noon hour. Two by two, the gin players made their way to their respective seats, followed by other diners.

Just before lunch, Mr. Hogan signaled for me to come to his table. When I arrived he asked me, "Just what do you shoot?"

"My best scores have been a few sixty-sixes, many sixty-sevens, and still more sixty-eights, but these courses I'm playing aren't Oakmont."

"Well they (the PGA tour players) are not playing Oakmont either or they wouldn't be shooting the scores they are shooting." Then leaning toward me he asked, "Have you ever played Oakmont?"

I thought, "Wow, here I am with an opportunity to talk to Ben Hogan about playing Oakmont, the site of his fourth US Open victory." I wondered where he would say he gained the edge in that tournament. Would he say it was the brilliant fairway wood he hit on the long par three seventieth hole, or the perfectly hit driver which reached the short par four seventy-first hole in one for an easy birdie three, or the three hundred yard drive on the seventy-second hole followed by a five iron that ended up a few feet from the hole?

But the grill was filling up and I needed to keep moving.

I said, "No, I haven't," and moved on with my duties.

Lunch came and Mr. Hogan had his usual cup of navy bean soup, but this time he also had two strips of bacon. He finished his meal, followed by his standard cup of coffee, and then slipped off to get his hat and club before embarking on his walk. He returned to the grill about forty minutes later, seeming very much at peace from his hike.

After delivering his Chardonnay, I commented, "It looks nice out."

"Very nice," he replied.

I continued working the room. However, it was not long before Mr. Hogan called me over to his table.

"Yes, Mr. Hogan?"

With a compassionate expression he said, "I want to help you. I want to get you playing privileges here. Write down everything about you and what you've done with golf so I can talk intelligently about you to the club president, Gene Smyers. Do you need to take a cart?"

"No," I responded pointing to my slight paunch, "I need to get rid of this."

"You know there is a par three nine where you can practice," he added.

I realized that the area to which he was referring was where he used to practice. Having been privileged to watch him practice in that area on a couple of occasions, for me to chew up the well cultivated turf there would be akin to desecrating hallowed ground. I just nodded to his suggestion. Then, trying to get a handle on balancing practice time and practice rounds, I asked, "How often should I play?"

"Oh, get out for nine holes two or three

times a week," he instructed.

Then I said, "My problem is that I always try to hit the perfect shot."

He cautioned, "Well, don't get too fancy."

I went off for a few minutes to fashion a quick, ad hoc, resume, then returned and handed Mr. Hogan the piece of paper.

Before clocking out, I remained long enough to see him studying the information I had given him, his head buried in the paper, applying the same undivided attention and focus I had seen him use when he competed.

CHAPTER XV

Scheduling Conflicts

Tuesday, March 20, 1990

Charles and I discussed the weekend schedule. He said that he needed me Saturday. Although I had that Saturday morning and lunch available, I had a scheduling conflict for mid-afternoon. He said that would be fine, but then he said that he had received another complaint about me visiting with Mr. Hogan. "So from now on leave the man alone!" he declared.

As far as I was concerned, with this new edict, it was game over. I didn't want to put Charles in an awkward situation. But by the same token, there was no way I was going to alienate Mr Hogan. Besides, scheduling had become almost impossible. My main job had become a full time job, even requiring overtime hours on the busiest days. Plus, it was getting close to tournament season, and I needed to spend any "free time" preparing to compete. I was looking forward to trying to implement all of the tips I had received from Mr. Hogan.

I didn't really understand why Mr. Hogan had taken an interest in me. Perhaps it was my being an underdog. Perhaps it was because we were both slight in stature. Perhaps it was the small Texas town connection. Maybe it was the fact that I never wanted anything from him, having never asked for an autograph or special favor. Whatever the reason, I will be forever grateful.

It was tough realizing that my association with Shady Oaks was coming to an end. The past seven months had been a special time in my life. Not only the attention I had received from Mr. Hogan, but the other gracious members, the friendly staff, and the beautiful surroundings had made what was originally just a filler job a fulfilling experience. Had I been able to stay, I might have been able to get playing privileges or I might have ended up fired for fraternizing with Mr. Hogan. I would never know.

CHAPTER XVI

Last Day At
The Grill

Saturday, March 24, 1990

Saturday morning started out like gang busters. The weather was great and the grill was packed. We were so busy that I didn't get to spend any in-depth time with Mr. Hogan. There was never a lull in the action. On the whole, my last short day of working in the Shady Oaks Men's Grill was fairly uneventful.

CHAPTER XVII

Golf Courses in Heaven

Monday, April 9, 1990

I turned onto the clubhouse drive mid-afternoon on a sunny Monday, taking one last look at the beautiful grounds. Now that it was April, all of the trees and flowers were blooming, and the immaculately manicured fairways, greens, and tees had a deep green hue. I parked and savored the sweet scent of fresh cut grass blended with fragrant pollinating plants. Early spring had given the course an extra touch of grandeur.

I collected my last pay check, and then worked my way through the maze of corridors and into the Men's Grill. There was Mr. Hogan, at the large table in the southwest corner of the room. There was nothing capricious about Mr. Hogan. He was as constant as the morning sun. But this day was unlike the usual hubbub, with the traffic of members moving to and fro and the clattering of glasses on waiters' trays. Absent also were the lingering smells of garlic and butter from the melba toast, and the sweet aromas of navy beans and ham hocks.

It was Monday and the Men's Grill, as a facility, was closed. There was no waiter or cook; not even the gin players graced the halls of Shady Oaks on Mondays.

I approached Mr. Hogan's table where he sat in solitude, staring out the window with a solemn expression, clad in a brown suit I had never seen before. Although every time I had served him during prior months, his hair was always perfectly trimmed, today it looked like the day before he was to see his barber.

I spoke directly, "Hello, Mr. Hogan."

He turned from the window and looked at me. Flashing a big crinkled eyed grin he said, "Where have you been? I've missed you."

I didn't pull any punches when I explained, "It seems someone didn't like me talking to you."

He looked puzzled for a moment and then exclaimed, "They can't dictate who I talk to. I want to know who he is. I'll burn his country butt!"

I had a good idea who the distinguished member was, but there was no way I would tell him. As far as I was concerned, I was the one passing through, and the members were established, permanent figures who had literally paid their dues.

I further explained, "I am having to give up both of my part-time jobs anyways. My full time job has me busy, and I want to prepare for upcoming tournaments."

Then I added, "I'm really going to miss this place."

"You're not working here anymore?" he asked, as if he was just processing what I had said, and that this would probably be our last visit.

"No."

Changing the subject, I asked, "What did you think of the Masters? What did you think of Floyd dumping his shot on eleven in the hazard and opening the door for Faldo in the sudden death play off?"

"I didn't see the shot, and I didn't see the lie, or where the pin was, and besides, you can't get the proper perspective when you see it on TV."

"Well, I thought he must have miss hit or misjudged his second shot for it to end up in the water," I observed.

I had once read a quote from Mr. Hogan saying that at Augusta, if he hit the green in two on eleven, then he had pulled the shot since the percentage shot was to bail a little to the right of the green.

In appraising Floyd he offered, "I know he's a very fine player."

Changing the subject again, I said, "I don't

know how you did it, Mr. Hogan, I mean play-ing and practicing all of the time." I wasn't referring to his accomplishments or acco-lades, but only to his ability to focus on the task at hand without allowing distractions. Just trying to make ends meet and keep up with family obligations made it hard for me to put in the practice time required to be suc-cessful in golf.

Mr. Hogan made no comment, but gave me a look as if to say, "I knew what it would take, so I made it a priority, and just did it."

In my efforts to try to figure him out, I asked, "Did you go to bed early?"

"Not particularly."

"Did you watch TV?"

"Sometimes."

My feeling was that Mr. Hogan was from another era, and he was somewhat still in that era, almost as if he were in a time warp.

Finally he repeated his motto, "It takes a long time, twelve hour days, seven days a week."

"There is his secret," I thought, "he wasn't satisfied with just being superb. He sought perfection!"

In reiterating his wise axioms from our earlier sessions he said, "You must be able to read a course. You're the general, son. When you read a course, you take into account the lies, the pin positions, the bunkers, and the slopes of the fairways and greens. Then you must be able to hit the shots the holes require. You practice these shots first on the practice tee, and then take them to the course."

I was reminded of another great ball striker, Moe Norman, who became an acquaintance of mine, who had said that the longest walk in golf was the walk from the practice tee to the first tee because when the gun goes off you have to be able to hit the shots that you rehearsed in practice.

Turning sharply, while pointing to the driving range, he said, "You go out there and you work your tail off, son."

"I've never thought of golf as work," I responded. "I hope there are golf courses in heaven."

His eyes lit up, animated with the hope of golf in Glory Land while nodding, almost giddy in approval.

He extended his hand. I reached and gripped it while we both grinned at each other. His hand seemed smaller and softer than I would have expected. In fact, he seemed more diminutive than what I remembered from just three weeks earlier. "Didn't the great baseball player, Ted Williams, once comment that when he shook Ben Hogan's hand it felt like five bands of steel?" I thought. But that was forty years earlier, and now he was entering his twilight years. Time marches on and is partial to no one. This would be my first and last time to shake the great man's hand.

CHAPTER XVIII

Back to
the Stunning
Reception

Monday, August 13, 1990

In the months following my days at the grill, I enjoyed some successes as well as setbacks. It was because of these setbacks that I was prompted to make one last trip to Shady Oaks on August 13th of 1990. Mr. Hogan had been so supportive when I last saw him, and I hoped he could help me do some tweaking of my game to get me over the hump.

I entered the grill through the glass door and immediately noticed Mr. Hogan sitting at his usual table alone with a cake that read "Happy Birthday Ben." He was the only soul in the room because it was another Monday, which was the club's day of rest. He stared out of the window engrossed in watching an amateur golf tournament.

I seemed to interrupt his concentration when I addressed him, "Hello Mr. Hogan. How are you?"

He turned his head in my direction and offered a closed lip smile and responded, "I'm fine, thanks."

While I had his attention, I began to discuss my recent tournament woes, "Well, after being encouraged by qualifying for the Texas Open, I drove for two days nonstop to the next tournament in Sioux Falls, South Dakota and nothing worked. I think it had something to do with my waggle. What do you think Mr. Hogan?"

His steely gray eyes seemed to bore right through me. He paused before he said, "I think we've been through this exercise before." He paused again. "I'm going to be curt with you. One day you are going to be an old man and still not know a goddamn thing. You get up at daybreak, and you hit balls until dark, and if you can't read a golf course you might as well be driving a goddamn gravel truck!"

The words seemed to roll out of his mouth in cadence with each stinging syllable rising in intonation until he finished. His diatribe caught me totally by surprise and mentally knocked me on my heels. I was puzzled, gripped by confusion.

I quickly tried to collect my thoughts and redirected the conversation like a sports reporter trying to get the big scoop. "Mr. Hogan, why was that sixth place finish at Oakland such a big moment in your career?"

His tone turned nostalgic as he recalled those days. "For me, $385 was a lot of money. I mean it wouldn't have been for some, but it was a lot for me. It was gas money!"

Then, quietly muttering, as if thinking to himself, Mr. Hogan said, "I'm trying to place you." He withdrew his eyes from mine and returned his attention outside to the juniors finishing up on the eighteenth green.

I thought to myself, "Holy crap. He doesn't remember me!" The picture became clearer. Although it had been a mere sixteen weeks since I had last seen him, he didn't recognize me! It was as if I were just some pestering golf pro trying to pick his brain - something for which he was known to have little patience. "Wow, I thought, this encounter is becoming as unbelievable as the momentous Sunday when he gave me the lesson!"

With that, I said, "Thank you Mr. Hogan."

He replied, "Good luck fella."

I was completely dumbfounded as I retreated from the table. However, in a strange way, I was actually relieved that he didn't remember me and was not snubbing me. He had been so gracious when we were seeing one another on a weekly basis. I wondered if I were to don a waiter's jacket if it might jog his memory. But at that point, I realized that the time we had spent together would be memories for me only, with no reciprocation. I was experiencing a whole gamut of emotions, but the underlying feeling was one of gratitude. Who knew that having a few food service skills would be equally as fortuitous as a golfing pedigree for gaining an audience with the great master?

CHAPTER XIX
Reflections

During that last visit, I had wanted to tell him that it was hard to use his preparation technique of playing two or three rounds at the various Hogan venues because some courses didn't even allow one practice round before the qualifier, but I refrained from making such comments when it was clear that he didn't remember me. As it turned out, although I was encouraged by the direction my game was headed, my run was almost over, and in fact, was totally finished two years later when my wife became disabled. But the advice I received from Mr Hogan has stuck with me. I have learned in golf and in life to treat each day as a challenge in which I try to make the most of the circumstances at play.

Often I have questioned why some young, budding future champion couldn't have been able to trade places with me during those inspiring and awakening months in 1990. For that matter, I would have given much for my encounter to have been seven years earlier, for it would have preceded my efforts on the Asian Tour. But the facts are that it happened when it happened, and only a few were lucky enough to have access and share moments with the elusive Ben Hogan.

It was obviously a real privilege getting a glimpse of his life at Shady Oaks during which was perhaps a punctuated moment of his latter years. It was a snap shot of the man that although, at the time, still had distinguishable vitality, had ceased his lifelong daily ritual of golf practice, which was a demonstrable part of his soul. So perhaps he was sort of letting go for life's twilight moment's preparation. Being prepared was what the man did best.

But for those friends who had known him and associated with him all those many years in the Men's Grill, he was so much more than a golfer. I once read that on his epitaph he would like to be remembered as a gentleman first, and a golfer second. While it is true that the character traits of persistence and perseverance which helped him overcome almost insurmountable odds, as well as his inexhaustible work ethic, are the traits that we golfers find so compelling, Ben, the gentleman, was the buffed and shined, finished product.

There is no question that after getting a look at Mr. Hogan, the man, I came to admire him all the more. It was heartening that he had such a humble spirit, and although the moments I spent in his service were short, the impact was profound.

Epilogue

Although many years have passed since 1990, when I was in service to the members of Shady Oaks Country Club, the memories are still as vivid as if they happened yesterday. The irony to this whole story is that had I not been in a career which job placement advisors categorize as a semi-skilled profession, I would have never met Mr. Hogan, let alone gotten to be on a friendly basis with him. But the truth is, I had always enjoyed this sort of work, so the story's setting placed me in my element.

Concerning my own efforts of trying to crack into the Hogan Tour, the closest I came was falling short by two strokes in the qualifier at the Reflection Ridge venue in Wichita, Kansas. During that round, I let this Hogan mantra resonate while grinding all day, "You must play the shot the hole dictates. You may not always pull it off, but you've got to try."

Bibliography

Davis, Martin. *The Greatest of Them All: The Legend of Bobby Jones.* Greenwich: The American Golfer, Inc., 1996.

Hogan, Ben. *Five Lessons: The Modern Fundamentals of Golf.* Ben Hogan, 1957. Reprint, New York: Simon & Schuster, Inc., 1985.

Hogan, Ben. *Power Golf.* Cranbury: A.S. Barnes & Company, Inc., 1948. Reprint, New York: Pocket Books, 1953.

Vicki Bryant, Curator of The Top of The Hill Terrace Museum, 2019.

Middlecoff, Cary. *The Golf Swing.* Englewood Cliffs: Prentice - Hall, Inc., 1969.

Nicklaus, Jack. *The Greatest Game of All: My Life in Golf.* New York: Simon & Schuster, 1969.

Acknowledgements

I would like to thank my brother, Gary Payne, for his impact in helping with phrasing. Thanks also to my industrious son, Raef Payne, for aid in design. Thanks to Brian Allen for encouraging me to write about my experiences with Mr. Hogan; to Regan White for his thoughtful editing; to Duac Lee and Don Collins for illustrations; and last, but not least, to my wife, Sherry, for her support and assistance with this project.

About the Author

Edward D. Payne is a golfer, writer, and entrepreneur, as well as a loving husband and father. He has a passion for history and expanding his knowledge of himself and the world around him. He currently resides in Arlington, Texas with Sharon Payne.

Made in the USA
Monee, IL
06 July 2020